Breakfast
IN FIVE

---

30 *low-carb* breakfasts

Up to **5** net carbs, **5** ingredients & **5** easy steps for every recipe

Vicky Ushakova & Rami Abramov

Table of Contents

Disclaimer

Tasteaholics, Inc. is not a medical company or organization. Our books provide information in respect to healthy eating, nutrition and recipes and are intended for informational purposes only. We are not nutritionists or doctors and the information in this book and our website is not meant to be given as medical advice. We are two people sharing our success strategies and resources and encouraging you to do further research to see if they will work for you too. Before starting any diet, you should always consult with your physician to rule out any health issues that could arise. Safety first, results second! Do not disregard professional medical advice or delay in seeking it because of this book.

Design & Photography

Cover design: Vicky & Rami Abrams

Interior design and layout: puroblanco.com

©Bigstock.com: barbaradudzinska, p.4; Valentina R., p.7; jirkaejc, p.8; egal, p.14; Madlen, p.17; jirkaejc, p.19; StephanieFrey, p.20; jirkaejc, p.22; Nika111, p.22; tashka2000, p.24; ersler, p.25; Yastremska, p.25; Maria Komar, p.26; janstarstud, p.28; dionisvera, p.29; Madlen, p.29; Natika, p.29; Kati Finell, p.32; Andregric, p.33; jirkaejc, p.34; silvy78, p.35; Kati Finell, p.36; Coprid, p.36; Madlen, p.38; kjekol, p.39; Valentina R., p.40; oysy, p.41; Maria Komar, p.42; Duplass, p.44; Yastremska, p.45; Inga Nielsen, p.46; Valentina R., p.46; elenathewise, p.47; jirkaejc, p.48; jirkaejc, p.48; dionisvera, p.50; n/a, p.51; Remus20, p.52; anphotos, p.52; Natika, p.53; Melica73, p.54; valio84sl, p.54; jirkaejc, p.56; lisovskaya, p.57; sommai, p.59; Gresei, p.60; margo555, p.62; Valentina R., p.63; Natika, p.64; pioneer111, p.65; Kovaleva Katerina, p.66; lenka, p.68; barbaradudzinska, p.70.

©Depositphotos.com: karandaev, p.6; zmaris, p.22; kornienkoalex, p.23; scukrov, p.23; rimglow, p.30; befehr, p.53; kozzi2, p.58; Goir, p.58.

©Envato.com: Timolina, p.11.

About This Book

This book was designed as a guide to help you kick start your ketogenic diet so you can lose weight, become healthy and have high energy levels every day.

Inside this book, you'll find the basics of the ketogenic diet, useful tips and delicious breakfast recipes.

Each recipe is only 5 grams of net carbs or fewer and can be made with just 5 ingredients! There's nothing better than that.

Eating low-carb doesn't require cutting out wholesome, nutritious foods or sacrificing taste — ever. We hand selected each ingredient to not only serve a delicious purpose but provide nutritious benefits.

Enjoy 30 delicious and easy low-carb breakfast recipes including pancakes, waffles, toast, muffins, hot pockets, tacos, cereals, sandwiches & soufflés that'll keep you full and excited for tomorrow's breakfast.

Let's get started!

Keto 101

What Is Keto?

The Ketogenic Diet

The ketogenic (or keto) diet is a low carbohydrate, high fat diet. Maintaining this diet is a great tool for weight loss but more importantly, according to an increasing number of studies, the keto diet reduces risk factors for diabetes, heart diseases, stroke, Alzheimer's, epilepsy, and more.[1-6]

On the keto diet, your body enters a metabolic state called ketosis. While in ketosis your body is using ketone bodies for energy instead of glucose. Ketone bodies are derived from fat and are a much more stable, steady source of energy than glucose, which is derived from carbohydrates.

Entering ketosis usually takes anywhere from 3 days to a week. Once you're in ketosis, you'll be using fat for energy instead of carbs. This includes the fat you eat and stored body fat.

While eating low carb, you'll lose weight easier, feel satiated longer and enjoy consistent energy levels throughout your day.

Testing for Ketosis

You can test yourself to see whether you've entered ketosis just a few days after you've begun the keto diet. Use a *ketone urine test strip* and it will tell you the level of ketone bodies in your urine. If the concentration is high enough and the test strip shows any hue of purple, you've successfully entered ketosis!

The strips take only a few seconds to show results and are the fastest and most affordable way to check whether you're in ketosis.

They are commonly found online or in most pharmacies for about ten U.S. dollars.

The Truth About Fat

You may be thinking, "eating a lot of fat is bad!" The truth is, dozens of studies with over 900,000 subjects have arrived at similar conclusions: eating saturated and monounsaturated fats has no effects on heart disease risks.[7,8]

Most fats are good and are essential to our health. Fats (fatty acids) and protein (amino acids) are essential for survival.

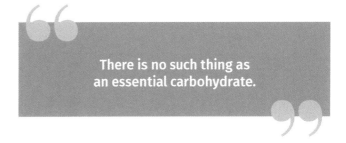

There is no such thing as an essential carbohydrate.

Fats are the most efficient form of energy and each gram of fat contains more than double the energy in a gram of protein or carbohydrates (more on that later).

The keto diet promotes eating fresh, whole foods like meat, fish, veggies, healthy fats and oils as well as greatly reducing processed and chemically treated foods the Standard American Diet (SAD) has so long encouraged.

It's a diet that you can sustain long-term and enjoy. After all, what's not to enjoy about bacon and eggs in the morning?

Calories & Macronutrients

How Calories Work

A calorie is a unit of energy. When something contains 100 calories, this describes the energy your body gets from consuming that food. Calorie consumption dictates weight gain/loss.

If you burn an average of 1,800 calories and eat 2,000 calories per day, you will gain weight.

If you do light exercise that burns an extra 300 calories per day, you'll burn 2,100 calories per day, putting you at a 100 calorie deficit. Eating at a deficit will cause you to lose weight because your body then taps into stored resources for the remaining energy it needs.

That being said, it's important to get the right balance of macronutrients every day so your body has the energy it needs.

What are Macronutrients?

Macronutrients (macros) are molecules that our bodies use to create energy – primarily fat, protein and carbs. These are found in all foods and are measured in grams (g) on nutrition labels.

tasteaholics.com/calculator

- **Fat** provides 9 calories per gram
- **Protein** provides 4 calories per gram
- **Carbs** provide 4 calories per gram
- **Alcohol** provides 7 calories per gram

Learn more at tasteaholics.com/macros.

Net Carbs

Most low carb recipes write net carbs when displaying their macros. Net carbs are total carbs minus dietary fiber and sugar alcohols. Since our bodies can't break these down into glucose, they don't count toward your total carb count.

Note: *Dietary fiber can be listed as soluble or insoluble.*

How Much Should You Eat?

On a keto diet, about 65 to 75 percent of the calories you consume daily should come from fat. About 20 to 30 percent should come from protein. The remaining 5 percent or so should come from carbohydrates.

Use the keto calculator on our website to figure out exactly how many calories and macros you should be eating every day!

It will ask for basic information including your weight, activity levels and goals then will instantly provide you with the total calories and grams of fat, protein and carbs that you should be eating each day.

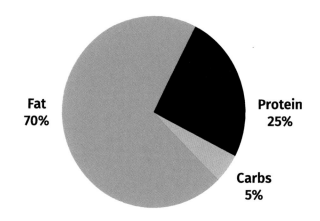

Note: *The calculator should be used as a general guideline. The results are based on your inputs and variables such as body fat percentage and basal metabolic rate are difficult to estimate correctly.*

A Nutritional Revolution

Carbs: What Exactly are They?

Carbohydrates (carbs) are found in things like starches, grains and foods high in sugar. This includes, but isn't limited to, bread, flour, rice, pasta, beans, potatoes, sugar, syrup, cereals, fruits, bagels and soda.

Our bodies break down carbs into glucose (a type of sugar) that they use for energy. Eating any kinds of carbs spikes blood sugar levels. The spike may happen faster or slower depending on the type of carb (based on the glycemic index), but the spike will still happen.

Blood sugar spikes cause strong insulin releases to combat these spikes. Constant insulin releases result in fat storage and insulin resistance. After many years, this cycle can lead to prediabetes, metabolic syndrome and even type 2 diabetes.[9]

In a world full of sugar, cereal, pasta, burgers, French fries and large sodas, you can see how carbs can easily be overconsumed.

> **Almost 1 in 10 adults in the U.S. have type 2 diabetes, nearly 4 times more than 30 years ago.**

Where We are Today

According to the 2014 report by the Centers for Diseases Control and Prevention (CDC), more than 1 in 3 adults in the U.S. (86 million people) have prediabetes, a condition in which blood glucose is always high. This commonly leads to type 2 diabetes and many other medical problems.[10]

Today, almost 1 in 10 people in the U.S. have type 2 diabetes compared to almost 1 in 40 in 1980.

Fat has been blamed as the bad guy and carbohydrates have been considered crucial and healthy. Companies have been creating low-fat and fat-free, chemical-laden alternatives of nearly every type of food in existence, yet diabetes and heart disease rates are still increasing.

Fat is Making a Comeback

Hundreds of studies have been conducted in the past ten years which have been corroborating the same data: that eating healthy fats is not detrimental to health and is, in fact, more beneficial than eating a diet high in carbohydrates.

We're starting to understand that carbs in large quantities are much more harmful than previously thought, while most fats are healthy and essential.

The nutritional landscape is changing. Low carb and similar dietary groups are growing and a nutritional revolution is beginning. We are beginning to realize the detrimental effects of our relationship with excess sugar and carbs.

The Basics: Benefits of Going Keto

Long-Term Benefits

Studies consistently show that those who eat a low carb, high fat diet rather than a high carb, low fat diet:

- Lose more weight and body fat[11–17]

- Have better levels of good cholesterol (HDL and large LDL)[18,19]

- Have reduced blood sugar and insulin resistance (commonly reversing prediabetes and type 2 diabetes)[20,21]

- Experience a decrease in appetite[22]

- Have reduced triglyceride levels (fat molecules in the blood that cause heart disease)[19,23]

- Have significant reductions in blood pressure, leading to a reduction in heart disease and stroke.[24]

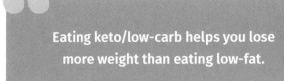
Day-to-Day Benefits

The keto diet doesn't only provide long-term benefits. When you're on keto, you can expect to:

- Lose body fat
- Have stable energy levels during the day
- Stay satiated after meals longer, with less snacking and overeating

Longer satiation and consistent energy levels are due to the majority of calories coming from fat, which is slower to digest and calorically denser.

Eating low carb also eliminates blood glucose spikes and crashes. You won't have sudden blood sugar drops leaving you feeling weak and disoriented.

Entering Ketosis

The keto diet's main goal is to keep you in nutritional ketosis all the time. If you're just getting started with your keto diet, you should eat up to 25 grams of carbs per day.

Once you're in ketosis for long enough (about 4 to 8 weeks), you become keto-adapted, or fat-adapted. This is when the glycogen stores in your muscles and liver are depleted, you carry less water weight, muscle endurance increases and your overall energy levels are higher.

Once keto-adapted, you can usually eat ≈50 grams of net carbs a day to maintain ketosis.

Type 1 Diabetes & Ketoacidosis

If you have type 1 diabetes, consult with your doctor before starting a keto diet. Diabetic ketoacidosis (DKA) is a dangerous condition that can occur if you have type 1 diabetes due to a shortage of insulin.

Steering Clear of the Keto Flu

What is the Keto Flu?

The keto flu happens commonly to keto dieters due to low levels of sodium and electrolytes and has flu-like symptoms including:

- Fatigue
- Headaches
- Cough
- Sniffles
- Irritability
- Nausea

It's important to note that this isn't the real flu! It's called keto flu due to similar symptoms but it is not at all contagious and doesn't actually involve a virus.

Why Does It Happen?

The main cause of the keto flu is your body lacking electrolytes, especially sodium. When starting keto, you cut out lots of processed foods and eat more whole, natural foods. Although this is great, it causes a sudden drop in sodium intake.

> **The keto flu can be avoided by consuming enough electrolytes, especially sodium.**

In addition, reducing carbs reduces insulin levels, which reduces sodium stored in the kidneys.[25]

Between your reduced sodium intake and any stored sodium flushed by your kidneys, you end up being low on sodium and other electrolytes.

Ending the Keto Flu

The best way to avoid or end the keto flu is to add more sodium and electrolytes to your diet. Here are the most effective (and tasty) ways to get more sodium:

- Adding more salt to your food
- Drinking soup broth
- Eating plenty of salty foods like bacon and pickled vegetables

Try to eat more sodium as you start the keto diet to prevent the keto flu entirely. If you do get the keto flu, just remember that it'll go away quickly and you'll emerge a fat-burning machine!

Note: *For more information about the keto flu, read our full guide at tasteaholics.com/keto-flu/.*

Starting Keto

Part 1 — Out with the Old

Having tempting, unhealthy foods in your home is one of the biggest reasons for failure when starting any diet.

To maximize your chances of success, you need to remove as many unhealthy food triggers as you can. This crucial step will help prevent moments of weakness from ruining all your hard work.

If you aren't living alone, make sure to discuss with your family or housemates before throwing anything out. If some items are simply not yours to throw out, try to compromise and agree on a special location so you can keep them out of sight and out of mind.

Once your home is free of temptation, eating low carb is far less difficult and success is that much easier.

Starches and Grains

Get rid of all cereal, pasta, bread, rice, potatoes, corn, oats, quinoa, flour, bagels, rolls, croissants and wraps.

All Sugary Things

Throw away and forget all refined sugar, fruit juices, desserts, fountain drinks, milk chocolate, pastries, candy bars, etc.

Legumes

Discard or donate any beans, peas, and lentils.

Vegetable & Seed Oils

Stop using any vegetable oils and seed oils like sunflower, safflower, soybean, canola, corn and grapeseed oil. Get rid of trans fats like margarine.

Read Nutrition Labels

Check the nutrition labels on all your foods to see if they are high in carbs. There are hidden carbs in the unlikeliest of places (like ketchup and canned soups)! Try to avoid buying products with dozens of incomprehensible ingredients as well. Less is usually healthier.

For example:

> Deli ham can have 2 or 3 grams of sugar per slice as well as many added preservatives and nitrites!

Nutrition Facts

Serving Size   1 Cup (53g/1.9 oz.)
Servings Per Container   About 8

Amount Per Serving

Calories 190		Calories from Fat 25

	% Daily Value*
Total Fat 3g	5%
Saturated Fat 0g	0%
Trans Fat 0g	
Cholesterol 0mg	0%
Sodium 100mg	4%
Potassium 300mg	9%
Total Carbohydrate 37g	12%
Dietary Fiber 8g	32%
Soluble Fiber ?	
Insoluble Fibe?	
Sugars 13g	
Protein 9g	14%

Vitamin A 0%		C 0%
Calcium 4%		10%
Phosphorus 10%		0%

* Percent Daily Values are based o
Your daily values may be higher o

Always check the serving sizes against the carb counts. Manufacturers can sometimes recommend inconceivably small serving sizes to seemingly reduce calorie and carb numbers.

At first glance, something may be low in carbs, but a quick comparison to the serving size can reveal the product is mostly sugar. Be diligent!

Part 2 — In with the New!

Now that you've cleaned out everything you don't need, it's time to restock your pantry and fridge with delicious and wholesome, keto-friendly foods that will help you lose weight, become healthier, and feel amazing!

General Products to Have

With these basics in your home, you'll always be ready to make healthy, keto-friendly meals.

- Lots of water, coffee, and unsweetened tea
- Stevia and erythritol (sweeteners)
- Condiments like mayonnaise, mustard, pesto, and sriracha
- Broths (beef, chicken, bone)
- Pickles and other fermented foods
- Seeds and nuts (chia seeds, flaxseeds, pecans, almonds, walnuts, macadamias, etc.)

Meat, Fish & Eggs

Just about every type of fresh meat and fish is good for keto including beef, chicken, lamb, pork, salmon, tuna, etc. Eat grass-fed and/or organic meat and wild-caught fish whenever possible.

Eat as many eggs as you like, preferably organic from free-range chickens.

Vegetables

Eat plenty of non-starchy veggies including asparagus, mushrooms, broccoli, cucumber, lettuce, onions, peppers, cauliflower, tomatoes, garlic, Brussels sprouts and zucchini.

Dairy

You can eat full-fat dairy like sour cream, heavy whipping cream, butter, cheeses and unsweetened yogurt.

Although not dairy, unsweetened almond milk and coconut milk are both good milk substitutes.

Stay away from regular milk, skim milk and sweetened yogurts because they contain a lot of sugars. Avoid all fat-free and low-fat dairy products.

Oils and Fats

Olive oil, avocado oil, butter and bacon fat are great for cooking and consuming. Avocado oil is best for searing due to its very high smoke point (520°F).

Fruits

Berries like strawberries, blueberries, and raspberries are allowed in small amounts. Avocados are also great because they're low carb and very high in fat!

Alcohol

Most 40% liquors (vodka, whiskey, cognac, gin, tequila, etc.) are 0-carb. Dry wines are 3–6 grams of carbs per 5 oz. serving. Light beers are 2–6 grams of carbs per 12 oz. serving.

Recipes

Notes

- We use large eggs in all our recipes. If yours are a different size, know that this will affect the nutrition slightly.

- The sugar-free, low-carb protein powder we use is *Isopure* Vanilla and *Isopure* Chocolate.

- Try to find the most natural peanut and almond butter brands you can. The ingredients listed should be, at most, 2 ingredients long.

- If you don't have stevia, feel free to substitute your favorite sugar-free sweetener like erythritol, xylitol, Splenda, etc. Add a little at a time and work your way up to taste.

  - You can order erythritol online by visiting tasteaholics.com/erythritol.

- The mozzarella cheese in each recipe is a low-moisture, part-skim, shredded mozzarella cheese; not fresh mozzarella.

- If you see the abbreviation "SF" it is short for "sugar-free".

  - For example, "SF Maple Syrup" means we used *Walden Farms* or *Sukrin Gold* syrup, both of which are sugar-free brands.

- If you're not a fan of spicy foods, feel free to leave out ingredients like jalapeño peppers, hot sauce, red pepper flakes, etc.

- The marinara sauce we use in all our recipes is of the brand *Rao's Homemade Sauces*. They are a low-sugar or no sugar added tomato sauce maker which can be found in many supermarkets. You can also choose to make your own from scratch or use any low-sugar tomato sauce you have on hand.

- A food scale is a must if you're counting calories and macros. Many of our ingredients are listed by weight to provide accurate nutritional data.

Low-Carb Friendly Seasonings

The following herbs and spices may be used in any of our recipes should you wish to add them.

They are all low-carb though we suggest limiting them to under a tablespoon to stay within your daily goals. It's more than enough to add their delicious flavors to your dishes without putting you over your carb limit!

☐ Salt

☐ Pepper

☐ Paprika

☐ Cayenne

☐ Thyme

☐ Basil

☐ Oregano

☐ Parsley

☐ Rosemary

☐ Tarragon

☐ Sage

☐ Cumin

☐ Red pepper flakes

☐ Sesame seeds

How to Make Cloud Buns

Whether you call them Oopsie Rolls, Cloud Bread or Cloud Buns, you'll see them being used in a few of our breakfast recipes. They can be made using only 3 ingredients so they're perfect for our purposes. We recommend making a batch the night before or on Sunday to have for the week.

Store them in an air-tight container in the refrigerator with some parchment paper in between each bun for up to a week. You can also freeze them in a single layer on a baking sheet, then transfer into a large Ziploc bag and store for up to 2 months.

Nutrition per Cloud Bun

50 calories | Makes 10–12 Cloud Buns

▍ 4 grams of fat

▍ 2.5 grams of protein

▍ 0.7 grams of carbs

🕑 **Prep Time: 10 mins | Cook Time: 30 mins**

Ingredients

- 3 large eggs
- 3 oz. cream cheese, cubed
- ⅛ tsp. cream of tartar or ⅛ tsp. baking powder

Instructions

1. Preheat the oven to 300°F.
2. Separate the eggs into two mixing bowls.
3. Beat the egg whites with a clean, electric hand mixer until foamy.
4. Add cream of tartar (or baking powder) and beat until opaque and shiny.
5. Beat the cream cheese and egg yolks until well combined and pale in color.
6. Fold the egg whites into the egg yolk mixture very gently.
7. Spoon ¼ cup at a time onto a parchment paper-lined baking sheet about 1–2 inches apart and bake for 30 minutes.
8. Let cool completely before removing and enjoying.

Blueberry Almond Pancakes

Low sugar, gluten-free and dairy-free pancakes that are incredibly easy to make. They taste and feel so close to the real thing!

Nutrition

500 calories per serving | Makes 2 servings

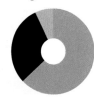

42 grams of fat	
20 grams of protein	
5 grams of net carbs	

Ingredients

- 1 cup almond flour
- 3 large eggs
- 1 ½ tsp. baking powder
- 50 grams frozen blueberries
- 2 tbsp. unsalted butter

Instructions

1. Combine almond flour, eggs, baking powder and a pinch of salt. Whisk until creamy. Thin out the batter with 1–2 tablespoons of water.
2. Heat a griddle and pour the batter to make 6, 5-inch pancakes. Add blueberries to each one.
3. Cook until you see bubbles forming on top, flip and cook again until golden brown.
4. Serve with butter and enjoy!

Avocado Cloud Toast

You, too, can have toast in the mornings! Topped with tangy mayo, a juicy slice of tomato and creamy avocado! Total perfection.

Nutrition

535 calories per serving | Makes 2 servings

52 grams of fat

6 grams of protein

3 grams of net carbs

🕐 **Prep Time: 5 mins | Cook Time: 0 mins**

Ingredients

- 4 Cloud Buns (see p. 30)
- 8 tbsp. mayonnaise
- 4 large tomato slices
- 1 large avocado
- Salt & pepper to taste

Instructions

1. Prepare the Cloud Buns recipe on page 28 the night before. Toast 4 buns until golden.
2. Open and pit the avocado. Cut it into quarters and slice them lengthwise.
3. Add 2 tablespoons of mayonnaise, a slice of tomato and 1 quarter of the sliced avocado to each toasted cloud bun.
4. Sprinkle with salt and pepper and enjoy!

Mediterranean Shakshuka

Poaching your eggs in marinara sauce makes a great, flavorful breakfast that's unusual, yet warm and inviting. Try it with feta and olives!

Nutrition

300 calories per serving | Makes 2 servings

22 grams of fat

18 grams of protein

5 grams of net carbs

Ingredients

- 1 cup marinara sauce
- 4 large eggs
- 2 oz. feta cheese
- 10 olives, chopped
- Fresh parsley

Instructions

1. Heat up the marinara sauce in a small skillet on high heat. Once the marinara is hot, crack the eggs in, spaced evenly apart.
2. Crumble the feta and chopped olives over the top of the eggs.
3. Bake at 400°F for about 10 minutes or until the eggs are slightly set on top.
4. Sprinkle with fresh parsley, let cool lightly and enjoy!

Loaded Butter Coffee

When you don't have time for a full breakfast but want something that'll keep you full for hours, wake up to this recipe!

Nutrition

490 calories per serving | Makes 1 serving

49 grams of fat	
3 grams of protein	
1 gram of net carbs	

⏱ **Prep Time: 5 mins | Cook Time: 0 mins**

Ingredients

- 1 cup brewed coffee (or 1 shot espresso)
- 1 tbsp. coconut oil
- 1 tbsp. unsalted butter
- ¼ cup heavy cream
- 1 large egg yolk

Instructions

1. Add your favorite brewed coffee or shot of espresso (+ some water) into a blender.
2. Add in the coconut oil, butter, heavy cream and egg yolk.
3. Blend on high until well combined and frothy. Do not skip blending this recipe or the oils will pool up at the top of coffee instead of emulsifying in it.
4. Sweeten if desired and enjoy!

Maple Pecan Porridge

A good sugar-free maple syrup is great to have around to sweeten low-carb treats — like this warm, filling maple pecan porridge!

Nutrition

390 calories per serving | Makes 2 servings

- 37 grams of fat
- 8 grams of protein
- 5 grams of net carbs

Ingredients

- ¼ cup flaxseed meal
- ¼ cup coconut flour
- ½ tsp. ground cinnamon
- 3 oz. pecans, toasted
- ¼ cup sugar-free maple syrup

Instructions

1. Heat 2 cups of water in a small pot.
2. Once steamy, add flaxseed meal, coconut flour and cinnamon to it. Stir until combined and cook until the whole thing has thickened.
3. Divide into bowls and garnish with whole or chopped toasted pecans.
4. Drizzle with sugar-free maple syrup and enjoy! (See page 34 for maple syrup recommendations.)

Savory Bacon Pancakes

Not your ordinary pancakes! These bacon pancakes are savory, salty and hearty — perfect for a super filling and unexpected breakfast.

Nutrition

420 calories per serving | Makes 2 servings

32 grams of fat

25 grams of protein

4 grams of net carbs

Ingredients

- 4 oz. cream cheese
- 4 large eggs
- ½ tsp. baking powder
- 6 strips bacon
- 2 stalks green onion, chopped

Instructions

1. Cook the bacon until desired crispiness, then chop it into bits.
2. Add cream cheese, eggs and baking powder into a small blender and blend until smooth.
3. Add the bacon bits and chopped green onion and stir them in.
4. Pour the batter onto a pan or griddle on medium heat and cook until bubbles start to form at the surface, about 3–5 minutes.
5. Flip and cook for another minute. Serve with a sprinkle of green onion and enjoy!

Blueberry Coconut Muffin

Soft, moist and coconutty! This blueberry coconut muffin for one is the perfect recipe to take with you on-the-go or enjoy at home.

Nutrition

375 calories per serving | Makes 1 serving

- 33 grams of fat
- 7 grams of protein
- 5 grams of net carbs

Ingredients

- 2 tbsp. coconut flour
- ½ tsp. baking powder
- 2 tbsp. coconut oil
- 1 large egg
- 15 grams blueberries, fresh or frozen

Instructions

1. Combine the coconut flour and baking powder in a bowl and whisk to get rid of any clumps.
2. Add in coconut oil and an egg and stir until well combined.
3. Fold in a few blueberries and a pinch of salt.
4. Pour into a lightly greased muffin tin and bake at 350°F for about 18 minutes.
5. Let cool completely before enjoying.

Ham, Egg & Cheese 'wich

What could be simpler than a sandwich? Toast up a couple of Cloud Buns and top them with whatever you please!

Nutrition

523 calories per serving | Makes 2 servings

	44 grams of fat
	28 grams of protein
	4 grams of net carbs

🕐 **Prep Time: 5 mins | Cook Time: 5 mins**

Ingredients

- 4 Cloud Buns (see p. 30)
- 4 tbsp. mayonnaise
- 2 large eggs
- 2 slices pepper jack cheese
- 4 oz. black forest ham, sliced

Instructions

1. Prepare the Cloud Buns recipe the night before. Toast 4 buns until golden.
2. Fry the eggs and season with salt and pepper.
3. Add 2 tablespoons of mayonnaise to 2 cloud buns and add a slice of pepper jack cheese.
4. Lay a fried egg over each slice of cheese.
5. Add black forest ham and top with another cloud bun. Enjoy!

Chocolate Chip Waffles

Feel like a kid again with our healthier chocolate chip waffles. They're low-carb, sugar-free & gluten-free. Perfect for any morning!

Nutrition

400 calories per serving | Makes 2 servings

▌ 26 grams of fat

▌ 34 grams of protein

▌ 4.5 grams of net carbs

Ingredients

- 62 grams low-carb protein powder (see p. 28)
- 2 large eggs, separated
- 2 tbsp. melted butter
- 50 grams cacao nibs (or SF chocolate chips)
- Sugar-free maple syrup to taste

Instructions

1. Whisk the egg whites until stiff peaks form.
2. Combine protein powder, egg yolks and melted butter in a mixing bowl and whisk.
3. Gently fold in the egg whites, being very careful not to deflate them, then add cacao nibs (or sugar-free chocolate chips) and a pinch of salt.
4. Grease a waffle iron and cook batter according to the manufacturer's instructions until lightly golden. Do not overcook the waffles!
5. Serve with sugar-free maple syrup and enjoy!

Cauliflower Hash Browns

What can't cauliflower do? It's a magical vegetable that can take the form of many of your favorite foods. Hash browns are no exception!

Nutrition

116 calories per serving | Makes 2 servings

- 8.5 grams of fat
- 5.5 grams of protein
- 4 grams of net carbs

Ingredients

- 150 grams cauliflower
- 1 large egg
- 1 stalk green onion
- ½ tsp. garlic powder
- ¼ cup sour cream

Instructions

1. Rice the cauliflower using a cheese grater into small pieces. Combine with the egg, chopped green onion and garlic powder in a mixing bowl.
2. With your hands, form flat patties about 4 inches in diameter.
3. In a well greased pan on low-medium heat, fry until golden brown on both sides. This should take about 5–8 minutes per side.
4. Enjoy with a dollop of sour cream.

Breakfast Tacos

Breakfast tacos are the perfect Sunday treat for your family! A simple cheese shell is all it takes to have a fun, Spanish-style breakfast.

Nutrition

600 calories per serving | Makes 2 servings

| | 43 grams of fat |
| 46 grams of protein |
| 5 grams of net carbs |

⏱ **Prep Time: 10 mins | Cook Time: 15 mins**

Ingredients

- 1 ½ cups shredded mozzarella (see p. 28)
- 6 large eggs
- 4 strips bacon
- ½ avocado, cubed
- 1 roma tomato, chopped

Instructions

1. Add a ¼ cup of shredded mozzarella at a time to a hot pan. Let it melt and brown. Flip and let the other side brown.
2. Gently remove the cheese using a spatula and drape it over a wooden spoon set on a bowl to cool into a taco shape. Repeat for all the cheese.
3. Cook the bacon and chop into bits. Scramble the eggs and season them with salt and pepper.
4. Add bacon bits, eggs, avocado, tomato and a bit more cheese into the shells and enjoy!

Morning Hot Pockets

Imagine the possibilities when you perfect these amazingly versatile hot pockets. You can fill them with just about anything you like!

Nutrition

455 calories per serving | Makes 2 servings

- 38 grams of fat
- 25 grams of protein
- 3 grams of net carbs

⏱ **Prep Time: 20 mins | Cook Time: 20 mins**

Ingredients

- ¾ cup shredded mozzarella (see p. 28)
- ⅓ cup almond flour
- 2 large eggs
- 2 tbsp. unsalted butter
- 3 slices bacon, cooked

Instructions

1. Melt the shredded mozzarella and add in the almond flour. Stir until well combined, microwaving again if necessary. Roll the dough out between 2 sheets of parchment paper until about a ½ cm thick.
2. Scramble the eggs in the butter and lay them with the cooked bacon slices along the center of the flattened dough.
3. Fold the dough over itself and seal the seam by pinching the edges. Add some holes on top for releasing some steam while baking.
4. Bake, seam down, at 400°F for about 20 minutes or until golden brown and firm and dry to the touch.

Strawberries & Cream Shake

Shakes and smoothies have a very special place in a busy person's life. Our strawberries & cream shake is sweet and light, yet quite filling!

Nutrition

430 calories per serving | Makes 2 servings

49 grams of fat

3 grams of protein

5 grams of net carbs

Ingredients

- 80 grams strawberries
- 1 cup unsweetened almond milk
- 1 cup heavy cream
- ½ tsp. vanilla extract
- 10 drops liquid stevia (optional)

Instructions

1. Rinse and hull the strawberries.
2. Pour the almond milk and heavy cream into a blender.
3. Throw the strawberries in along with the vanilla extract and stevia, if desired.
4. Blend on high until completely combined and creamy.
5. Enjoy!

On-The-Go Quiches

These quiches are great to make on Sundays to enjoy all week. They keep well in the fridge and can be reheated at work or school!

Nutrition

340 calories per serving | Makes 4 servings

- 24 grams of fat
- 20 grams of protein
- 5 grams of net carbs

⏱ **Prep Time: 10 mins | Cook Time: 25 mins**

Ingredients

- 4 oz. roma tomato
- 2 oz. red onion
- 6 oz. white or brown mushrooms
- 12 large eggs
- ½ cup heavy cream

Instructions

1. Dice the roma tomato, red onion and mushrooms and cook them on medium heat until the onion is translucent, about 8 minutes.
2. Meanwhile, whisk together the eggs and heavy cream in a large bowl until very pale.
3. Add the cooked veggies to the bowl and stir.
4. Add the batter evenly into a lightly greased muffin tin and bake at 350°F for 25 minutes.
5. Let cool completely before removing. Store in an airtight container in the refrigerator and warm them up before enjoying. They may be frozen to enjoy later!

Coconut Macadamia Bars

Breakfast bars are a great way to save some time in the mornings. Make a batch and keep them in the fridge at home or work all week!

Nutrition

375 calories per serving | Makes 5 servings

38 grams of fat	
7 grams of protein	
5 grams of net carbs	

⏱ **Prep Time: 10 mins** | **Passive Time: 12 hrs**

Ingredients

- 60 grams macadamia nuts
- ½ cup almond butter
- ¼ cup coconut oil, melted
- 6 tbsp. unsweetened shredded coconut
- 20 drops liquid stevia

Instructions

1. Pulse the macadamia nuts in a food processor until very fine.
2. Combine almond butter, coconut oil and coconut in a bowl. Add the nuts and stevia.
3. Mix thoroughly and pour the batter into a 9×9" parchment paper-lined baking dish.
4. Refrigerate overnight, slice and enjoy chilled.

Tip: *These bars work wonderfully frozen too!*

High Fiber, High Crunch Cereal

Missing your bowl of cereal in the mornings? Make your own that's high in fat, fiber and protein to keep you full and energized!

Nutrition

350 calories per serving | Makes 2 servings

- 30 grams of fat
- 11 grams of protein
- 5 grams of net carbs

🕐 **Prep Time: 5 mins | Cook Time: 5 mins**

Ingredients

- ½ cup unsweetened coconut flakes
- 2 oz. almonds, whole or chopped
- 2 tbsp. chia seeds
- 2 cups unsweetened almond milk
- 10 drops liquid stevia (optional)

Instructions

1. Start by toasting the coconut flakes in the oven at 350°F for 5 minutes, stirring or rotating occasionally to avoid burning.
2. Combine almonds, chia seeds and the toasted coconut flakes in 2 serving bowls.
3. Pour the almond milk over both and sweeten with stevia if desired.
4. Stir and enjoy!

Goat Cheese Frittata

Frittatas are great for a large family breakfast or even for dinner. And if you've got leftover veggies, this is the recipe to make to use them all up!

Nutrition

410 calories per serving | Makes 4 servings

32 grams of fat

26 grams of protein

4 grams of net carbs

Ingredients

- 16 spears asparagus
- 4 oz. white or brown mushrooms
- 12 large eggs
- ½ cup heavy cream
- 4 oz. goat cheese or feta cheese

Instructions

1. Cut the fibrous ends off the asparagus and slice the mushrooms. Cook them in a well-oiled 10" cast iron skillet until slightly browned and softened.
2. Whisk the eggs and heavy cream until very pale. Season with salt and pepper.
3. Add the beaten eggs into the cast iron skillet and crumble the goat cheese or feta cheese on top.
4. Bake at 375°F for 15 minutes, let cool lightly and enjoy.

Breakfast Burritos

You don't have to go out for burritos — you can make them at home with some creamy scrambled eggs and spicy jalapeños!

Nutrition

320 calories per serving | Makes 2 servings

25 grams of fat

18 grams of protein

2 grams of net carbs

Ingredients

- 2 tbsp. butter or coconut oil
- 6 large eggs
- 1 roma tomato, diced
- Sliced pickled jalapeños, to taste
- 2 large butter lettuce leaves

Instructions

1. Melt the butter and scramble the eggs in it on medium heat until they're just almost cooked throughout. Take the pan off the heat to let the eggs finish cooking.
2. Add tomato and jalapeño slices to the butter lettuce leaves. Then add the scrambled eggs and season with salt and pepper.
3. Roll up the butter lettuce leaves and enjoy now or pack away for later!

Powerhouse Shake

If you're constantly running out the door, make yourself a breakfast in a bottle by combining caffeine, fat & protein!

⊙ **Prep Time: 8 mins | Cook Time: 0 mins**

Nutrition

425 calories per serving | Makes 2 servings

| 38 grams of fat

▮ 26 grams of protein

| 1 gram of net carbs

Ingredients

- 2 espresso shots
- 62 grams low-carb protein powder (see p. 28)
- ½ cup heavy cream
- 2 tbsp. coconut oil
- ½ tsp. ground cinnamon

Instructions

1. Pour the brewed espresso shots into a blender along with the protein powder (flavor of your choice), heavy cream, coconut oil and cinnamon.
2. Add about a cup of ice cubes, sweeten if desired, and blend on high until creamy and frothy.
3. Pour into a couple of mason jars with some more ice to take breakfast with you on-the-go.

Peanut & Cacao Nib Pudding

Make-ahead recipes just got easier. With only
5 ingredients, this chia seed pudding is full of flavor,
fiber and will save you precious minutes!

Nutrition

280 calories per serving | Makes 2 servings

20 grams of fat

9 grams of protein

5 grams of net carbs

Ingredients

- 1 ½ cups unsweetened almond milk
- 2 tbsp. chia seeds
- 2 tbsp. peanut butter (or almond butter)
- 10 drops liquid stevia
- 30 grams cacao nibs (or SF chocolate chips)

Instructions

1. The night before, combine the almond milk, chia
   seeds, peanut butter (or almond butter) and
   liquid stevia in a mixing bowl and whisk until the
   nut butter is well incorporated.
2. Transfer to a serving dish and cover with plastic
   wrap. Refrigerate overnight.
3. In the morning, top with cacao nibs (or sugar-free
   chocolate chips) and enjoy!

Spinach & Feta Scramble

Feta really gives scrambled eggs a great flavor and texture. The spinach gives you a boost of vitamins right when you wake up!

Nutrition

465 calories per serving | Makes 2 servings

36 grams of fat

29 grams of protein

2 grams of net carbs

Ingredients

- 2 tbsp. unsalted butter
- 2 cups fresh spinach
- 4 strips bacon
- 6 large eggs
- 2 oz. feta cheese

Instructions

1. Melt the butter in a pan and cook the spinach until wilted. In another pan, cook the bacon strips until desired crispiness.
2. Whisk the eggs in a small bowl and add them to the hot pan with the spinach.
3. Stir continuously until almost fully cooked, then crumble the feta into the pan.
4. Season with salt and pepper and remove from the heat to continue cooking all the way.
5. Serve with the bacon strips and enjoy!

Sweet Raspberry Porridge

This sweet raspberry porridge is the perfect recipe for cold winter mornings. It can even be ready before your coffee finishes brewing!

Nutrition

333 calories per serving | Makes 2 servings

- 32 grams of fat
- 6 grams of protein
- 5 grams of net carbs

🕐 **Prep Time: 5 mins | Cook Time: 8 mins**

Ingredients

- 2 cups unsweetened almond milk
- ¼ cup flaxseed meal
- ¼ cup coconut flour
- 60 grams raspberries
- 10 drops liquid stevia (optional)

Instructions

1. Heat the almond milk in a pan or small pot.
2. Once it's steamy, add in flaxseed meal and coconut flour. Stir until combined.
3. Add in the raspberries and cook until the whole mixture thickens and the raspberries stain the porridge.
4. Sweeten with stevia if desired and enjoy!

Cheesy Breakfast Pizza

Feeling like pizza? Don't let the time stop you! Make a quick, low-carb breakfast pizza and have yourself a hearty meal.

Nutrition

400 calories per serving | Makes 2 servings

	32 grams of fat
	26 grams of protein
	4 grams of net carbs

Ingredients

- 1 cup shredded mozzarella (see p. 28)
- ½ cup marinara sauce
- 2 large eggs, fried
- 2 oz. pepperoni, sliced
- 6 leaves fresh basil

Instructions

1. Spread the shredded mozzarella cheese onto a small frying pan on medium heat and let it melt, slightly browning on the bottom.
2. Add marinara sauce and the fried eggs. Top with pepperoni slices and cook covered for about 3 minutes.
3. Wedge a spatula under the cheese and gently remove the pizza. Top with fresh basil.

Low-Carb Granola

Granola is the perfect addition to your favorite breakfast. Enjoy this over a few spoonfuls of yogurt, a smoothie or as a bowl of cereal!

Nutrition

275 calories per serving | Makes 4 servings

▌ 25 grams of fat

▌ 10 grams of protein

▌ 3 grams of net carbs

Ingredients

- 1 cup whole almonds
- ¼ cup sunflower seeds
- ¼ cup pumpkin seeds
- 1 tbsp. coconut oil
- 15 drops liquid stevia

Instructions

1. Add the almonds, sunflower seeds and pumpkin seeds to a food processor and pulse a few times until they're roughly chopped.
2. Add coconut oil, stevia and a pinch of salt. Pulse again to coat evenly.
3. Spread the mixture onto a baking sheet in a thin layer and bake at 350°F for about 10 minutes or until golden brown.
4. Let cool and store in an airtight jar.

Tip: *Enjoy by itself like a cereal with unsweetened almond milk or crumble onto yogurt and smoothies!*

French Brie Soufflé

Fancy doesn't always mean difficult. Take our French brie soufflé, for example. Only 5 ingredients means you can dine like a king in no time!

Nutrition

525 calories per serving | Makes 2 servings

- 47 grams of fat
- 22 grams of protein
- 2 grams of net carbs

Ingredients

- ¼ cup unsalted butter, melted
- ¼ cup almond flour
- 4 large eggs, separated
- 2 oz. brie cheese, cubed
- ½ cup unsweetened almond milk

Instructions

1. Combine the butter and almond flour in a pan over low heat. Stir until thickened.
2. Whisk the egg yolks into the mixture as well as the brie and a pinch of salt. Stir well.
3. Add almond milk slowly, stirring until combined.
4. Beat the egg whites with a pinch of salt until stiff peaks form. Then, fold them very gently into the entire mixture.
5. Pour the batter into 4 well-greased ramekins, broil for 3 minutes then bake for 20 minutes at 400°F.

Choco-Peanut Butter Shake

Who can resist the heavenly combo of chocolate and peanut butter? Who's opposed to having it for breakfast? No one, that's who.

Nutrition

450 calories per serving | Makes 2 servings

| 33 grams of fat
| 33 grams of protein
| 4.5 grams of net carbs

🕐 **Prep Time: 5 mins | Cook Time: 0 mins**

Ingredients

- 2 cups unsweetened almond milk
- 62 grams low-carb chocolate protein powder (see p. 28)
- ¼ cup peanut butter
- 2 tbsp. coconut oil
- 10 ice cubes

Instructions

1. Combine all the ingredients in a blender.
2. Blend on high until everything is well combined.
3. Enjoy!

<u>Tip:</u> *If you don't have chocolate flavored protein powder, use vanilla or unflavored protein powder and add 1–2 tablespoons of unsweetened cocoa powder.*

Buttery Flaxseed Muffins

Flaxseeds give a great texture and add a ton of fiber to foods. They retain their natural moisture to make super juicy muffins!

Nutrition

205 calories per serving | Makes 4 servings

18 grams of fat

6 grams of protein

3 grams of net carbs

Ingredients

- 1 cup flaxseed meal
- 6 tbsp. granular erythritol
- 1 tsp. baking powder
- 2 large eggs
- ¼ cup unsalted butter, melted

Instructions

1. Combine the flaxseed meal, erythritol and baking powder and whisk well.
2. Add in the eggs and melted butter. Stir until well combined.
3. Pour into a lightly greased muffin tin and bake at 350°F for about 12 minutes.
4. Enjoy with some more butter!

Poached Eggs & Greens

A salad-inspired breakfast can be a refreshing break from the cooked, fried and baked breakfasts you may be used to.

Nutrition

400 calories per serving | Makes 2 servings

- 32 grams of fat
- 22 grams of protein
- 3 grams of net carbs

🕐 **Prep Time: 10 mins | Cook Time: 15 mins**

Ingredients

- 4 large eggs
- 6 strips bacon
- ¼ red onion, sliced
- 2 handfuls baby spinach
- ¼ tsp. paprika

Instructions

1. Gently poach the eggs in lightly boiling water for about 3 minutes each.
2. Cook the bacon strips and the red onion together until crispy.
3. Chop the bacon strips and add them and the red onion onto a bed of fresh baby spinach.
4. Pour a tablespoon of bacon grease onto each salad as a dressing. Season with salt and pepper and toss well.
5. Add the poached eggs on top and a sprinkle of paprika. Enjoy!

Pepper Bacon Omelet

This open-faced pepper bacon omelet is quick to make and has tons of flavor. If you've never tried mayo in an omelet, here's your chance!

Nutrition

475 calories per serving | Makes 2 servings

| 36 grams of fat
| 32 grams of protein
| 3 grams of net carbs

⏱ Prep Time: 5 mins | Cook Time: 15 mins

Ingredients

- 4 strips bacon
- ½ red bell pepper, chopped
- 6 large eggs, beaten
- 2 tbsp. mayonnaise
- ¼ cup shredded mozzarella (see p. 28)

Instructions

1. Cook bacon on medium heat on one side until crispy.
2. Flip the bacon and add chopped bell pepper in to cook in the bacon grease.
3. After that has cooked, set it all aside on a plate and chop the bacon into bits.
4. Add the eggs into the hot bacon grease and let cook halfway, scrambling them slightly.
5. Add the bell pepper, bacon bits, mayonnaise (spread lightly around the omelet) and cover with shredded mozzarella on top. Cook covered for about 5 minutes.
6. Season with salt and pepper. Enjoy!

Chorizo Breakfast Bake

These quick little cups of deliciousness will soon become your favorite breakfast recipe! They're savory, warm and quite filling!

Nutrition

418 calories per serving | Makes 2 servings

- 32 grams of fat
- 27 grams of protein
- 3 grams of net carbs

Ingredients

- ¼ red bell pepper, finely chopped
- ¼ green bell pepper, finely chopped
- 80 grams chorizo sausage, cooked
- ½ cup shredded mozzarella (see p. 28)
- 4 large eggs

Instructions

1. Cook the red and green bell peppers in a lightly oiled pan until soft. Slice the chorizo sausage into bite-sized pieces.
2. Lightly grease 4 ramekins and add the peppers, sausage and shredded mozzarella.
3. Crack an egg onto each ramekin and season with salt and pepper.
4. Bake for 12 minutes at 350°F and enjoy!

Thank You

Our hopes are that some of these keto cocktails will become staples in your life, helping you stay healthy and enjoy your ketogenic diet.

If you have questions, suggestions or any other feedback, please don't hesitate to contact us directly: hello@tasteaholics.com.

We answer emails every day and we'd love to hear from you. Each comment we receive is valuable and helps us in continuing to provide quality content.

Your direct feedback could be used to help others discover the benefits of going low carb!

If you have a success story, please send it to us! We're always happy to hear about our readers' success.

Thank you again and we hope you have enjoyed *Keto Cocktails in Five*!

— *Vicky & Rami Abrams*

About the Authors

Vicky & Rami Abrams co-founded Tasteaholics.com to provide an easy way to understand why the ketogenic diet is truly effective for weight loss and health management. They create recipes that are low-carb, high-fat and maximize flavor. The books in their *Keto in Five* series are wildly popular among the low-carb community due to their simplicity and efficacy.

Vicky and Rami's mission is to continue to improve their audience's health and outlook on life through diet and nutrition education. They are dedicated to helping change the detrimental nutritional guidelines in the United States and across the globe that have been plaguing millions of people over the last 40 years.

The duo travels the world to explore new cultures, cuisines and culinary techniques which they pass on through new recipes and content available on their website.

Personal Notes

Use these pages to write down any recipe notes and more delicious ideas.

References

1. Aude, Y., A. S, Agatston, F. Lopez-Jimenez, et al. "The National Cholesterol Education Program Diet vs a Diet Lower in Carbohydrates and Higher in Protein and Monounsaturated Fat: A Randomized Trial." JAMA Internal Medicine 164, no. 19 (2004): 2141–46. doi: 10.1001/archinte.164.19.2141. jamanetwork.com/journals/jamainternalmedicine/article-abstract/217514.

2. De Lau, L. M., M. Bornebroek, J. C. Witteman, A. Hofman, P. J. Koudstaal, and M. M. Breteler. "Dietary Fatty Acids and the Risk of Parkinson Disease: The Rotterdam Study." Neurology 64, no. 12 (June 2005): 2040–5. doi:10.1212/01.WNL.0000166038.67153.9F. www.ncbi.nlm.nih.gov/pubmed/15985568/.

3. Freeman, J. M., E. P. Vining, D. J. Pillas, P. L. Pyzik, J. C. Casey, and L M. Kelly. "The Efficacy of the Ketogenic Diet-1998: A Prospective Evaluation of Intervention in 150 Children." Pediatrics 102, no. 6 (December 1998): 1358–63. www.ncbi.nlm.nih.gov/pubmed/9832569/.

4. Hemingway, C, J. M. Freeman, D. J. Pillas, and P. L. Pyzik. "The Ketogenic Diet: A 3- to 6-Year Follow-up of 150 Children Enrolled Prospectively. Pediatrics 108, no. 4 (October 2001): 898–905. www.ncbi.nlm.nih.gov/pubmed/11581442/.

5. Henderson, S. T. "High Carbohydrate Diets and Alzheimer's Disease." Medical Hypotheses 62, no. 5 (2014): 689–700. doi:10.1016/j.mehy.2003.11.028. www.ncbi.nlm.nih.gov/pubmed/15082091/.

6. Neal, E.G., H. Chaffe, R. H. Schwartz, M. S. Lawson, N. Edwards, G. Fitzsimmons, A. Whitney, and J. H. Cross. "The Ketogenic Diet for the Treatment of Childhood Epilepsy: A Randomised Controlled Trial." Lancet Neurology 7, no. 6 (June 2008): 500–506. doi:10.1016/S1474-4422(08)70092-9. www.ncbi.nlm.nih.gov/pubmed/18456557.

7. Chowdhury, R., S. Warnakula, S. Kunutsor, F. Crowe, H. A. Ward, L. Johnson, et al. "Association of Dietary, Circulating, and Supplement Fatty Acids with Coronary Risk: A Systematic Review and Meta-Analysis." Annals of Internal Medicine 160 (2014): 398–406. doi:10.7326/M13-1788. annals.org/article.aspx?articleid=1846638.

8. Siri-Tarino, P. W., Q. Sun, F. B. Hu, and R. M. Krauss. "Meta-Analysis of Prospective Cohort Studies Evaluating the Association of Saturated Fat with Cardiovascular Disease." American Journal of Clinical Nutrition 91, no. 3 (March 2010): 535–46. doi:10.3945/ajcn.2009.27725. www.ncbi.nlm.nih.gov/pubmed/20071648.

9. "Prediabetes and Insulin Resistance," The National Institute of Diabetes and Digestive and Kidney Diseases. https://www.niddk.nih.gov/health-information/diabetes/types/prediabetes-insulin-resistance.

10. "National Diabetes Statistics Report," Centers for Disease Control and Prevention, 2014. http://www.cdc.gov/diabetes/pubs/statsreport14/national-diabetes-report-web.pdf.

11. Dyson, P. A., Beatty, S. and Matthews, D. R. "A low-carbohydrate diet is more effective in reducing body weight than healthy eating in both diabetic and non-diabetic subjects." Diabetic Medicine. 2007. 24: 1430–1435. http://onlinelibrary.wiley.com/doi/10.1111/j.1464-5491.2007.02290.x/full.

12. Christopher D. Gardner, PhD; Alexandre Kiazand, MD; Sofiya Alhassan, PhD; Soowon Kim, PhD; Randall S. Stafford, MD, PhD; Raymond R. Balise, PhD; Helena C. Kraemer, PhD; Abby C. King, PhD, "Comparison of the Atkins, Zone, Ornish, and LEARN Diets for Change in Weight and Related Risk Factors Among Overweight Premenopausal Women," JAMA. 2007;297(9):969-977. http://jama.jamanetwork.com/article.aspx?articleid=205916.

13. Gary D. Foster, Ph.D., Holly R. Wyatt, M.D., James O. Hill, Ph.D., Brian G. McGuckin, Ed.M., Carrie Brill, B.S., B. Selma Mohammed, M.D., Ph.D., Philippe O. Szapary, M.D., Daniel J. Rader, M.D., Joel S. Edman, D.Sc., and Samuel Klein, M.D., "A Randomized Trial of a Low-Carbohydrate Diet for Obesity – NEJM," N Engl J Med 2003; 348:2082-2090. http://www.nejm.org/doi/full/10.1056/NEJMoa022207.

14. JS Volek, MJ Sharman, AL Gómez, DA Judelson, MR Rubin, G Watson, B Sokmen, R Silvestre, DN French, and WJ Kraemer, "Comparison of Energy-restricted Very Low-carbohydrate and Low-fat Diets on Weight Loss and Body Composition in Overweight Men and Women," Nutr Metab (Lond). 2004; 1: 13. http://www.ncbi.nlm.nih.gov/pmc/articles/PMC538279/.

15. Y. Wady Aude, MD; Arthur S. Agatston, MD; Francisco Lopez-Jimenez, MD, MSc; Eric H. Lieberman, MD; Marie Almon, MS, RD; Melinda Hansen, ARNP; Gerardo Rojas, MD; Gervasio A. Lamas, MD; Charles H. Hennekens, MD, DrPH, "The National Cholesterol Education Program Diet vs a Diet Lower in Carbohydrates and Higher in Protein and Monounsaturated Fat," Arch Intern Med. 2004;164(19):2141-2146. http://archinte.jamanetwork.com/article.aspx?articleid=217514.

16. Bonnie J. Brehm, Randy J. Seeley, Stephen R. Daniels, and David A. D'Alessio, "A Randomized Trial Comparing a Very Low Carbohydrate Diet and a Calorie-Restricted Low Fat Diet on Body Weight and Cardiovascular Risk Factors in Healthy Women," The Journal of Clinical Endocrinology & Metabolism: Vol 88, No 4; January 14, 2009. http://press.endocrine.org/doi/full/10.1210/jc.2002-021480.

17. M. E. Daly, R. Paisey, R. Paisey, B. A. Millward, C. Eccles, K. Williams, S. Hammersley, K. M. MacLeod, T. J. Gale, "Short-term Effects of Severe Dietary Carbohydrate-restriction Advice in Type 2 Diabetes–a Randomized Controlled Trial," Diabetic Medicine, 2006; 23: 15–20. http://onlinelibrary.wiley.com/doi/10.1111/j.1464-5491.2005.01760.x/abstract.

18. Stephen B. Sondike, MD, Nancy Copperman, MS, RD, Marc S. Jacobson, MD, "Effects Of A Low-Carbohydrate Diet On Weight Loss And Cardiovascular Risk Factor In Overweight Adolescents," The Journal of Pediatrics: Vol 142, Issue 3: 253-258; March 2003. http://www.sciencedirect.com/science/article/pii/S0022347602402065.

19. William S. Yancy Jr., MD, MHS; Maren K. Olsen, PhD; John R. Guyton, MD; Ronna P. Bakst, RD; and Eric C. Westman, MD, MHS, "A Low-Carbohydrate, Ketogenic Diet versus a Low-Fat Diet To Treat Obesity and Hyperlipidemia: A Randomized, Controlled Trial," Ann Intern Med. 2004;140(10):769-777. http://annals.org/article.aspx?articleid=717451.

20. Grant D Brinkworth, Manny Noakes, Jonathan D Buckley, Jennifer B Keogh, and Peter M Clifton, "Long-term Effects of a Very-low-carbohydrate Weight-Loss Diet Compared with an Isocaloric Low-fat Diet after 12 Mo," Am J Clin Nutr July 2009 vol. 90 no. 1 23-32. http://ajcn.nutrition.org/content/90/1/23.long.

21. H. Guldbrand, B. Dizdar, B. Bunjaku, T. Lindström, M. Bachrach-Lindström, M. Fredrikson, C. J. Östgren, F. H. Nystrom, "In Type 2 Diabetes, Randomisation to Advice to Follow a Low-carbohydrate Diet Transiently Improves Glycaemic Control Compared with Advice to Follow a Low-fat Diet Producing a Similar Weight Loss," Diabetologia (2012) 55: 2118. http://link.springer.com/article/10.1007/s00125-012-2567-4.

22. Sharon M. Nickols-Richardson, PhD, RD, , Mary Dean Coleman, PhD, RD, Joanne J. Volpe, Kathy W. Hosig, PhD, MPH, RD, "Perceived Hunger Is Lower and Weight Loss Is Greater in Overweight Premenopausal Women Consuming a Low-Carbohydrate/High-Protein vs High-Carbohydrate/Low-Fat Diet," The Journal of Pediatrics: Vol 105, Issue 9: 1433–1437; September 2005. http://www.sciencedirect.com/science/article/pii/S000282230501151X.

23. Frederick F. Samaha, M.D., Nayyar Iqbal, M.D., Prakash Seshadri, M.D., Kathryn L. Chicano, C.R.N.P., Denise A. Daily, R.D., Joyce McGrory, C.R.N.P., Terrence Williams, B.S., Monica Williams, B.S., Edward J. Gracely, Ph.D., and Linda Stern, M.D., "A Low-Carbohydrate as Compared with a Low-Fat Diet in Severe Obesity, " N Engl J Med 2003; 348:2074-2081. http://www.nejm.org/doi/full/10.1056/NEJMoa022637.

24. Yancy WS Jr, Westman EC, McDuffie JR, Grambow SC, Jeffreys AS, Bolton J, Chalecki A, Oddone EZ, "A randomized trial of a low-carbohydrate diet vs orlistat plus a low-fat diet for weight loss," Arch Intern Med. 2010 Jan 25;170(2):136-45. http://www.ncbi.nlm.nih.gov/pubmed/20101008?itool=EntrezSystem2.PEntrez.Pubmed.Pubmed_ResultsPanel.Pubmed_RVDocSum&ordinalpos=2.

25. Swasti Tiwari, Shahla Riazi, and Carolyn A. Ecelbarger, "Insulin's Impact on Renal Sodium Transport and Blood Pressure in Health, Obesity, and Diabetes," American Journal of Physiology vol. 293, no. 4 (October 2, 2007): 974–984, http://ajprenal.physiology.org/content/293/4/F974.full.

Made in the USA
Coppell, TX
03 February 2020